101

ESSENTIAL TIPS

cat care

This book is our gift to you. It has been created to get you off to a great start, and ensure a long and happy life with your new kitten. Enclosed are all the essential tips you need to raise a healthy cat, including health signs and symptoms to look out for, plus the easiest ways you can protect your pet from parasite infestations and the illnesses that they can cause. Your team at VCA is here for you every step of the way for advice, care and support, so call or visit us any time.

AT VCA ANIMAL HOSPITALS, WE'VE GOT THEM COVERED

I protected him

IMPORTANT SAFETY INFORMATION: Paradyne is generally well tolerated. In studies, < 1% of cats and dogs experienced digestive upset. Approximately 1% of cats experienced temporary hair loss at the application site. Do not use in sick, weak, or underweight animals. For more information see the full Prescribing Information, or visit Vethical.com.

Paradyne®
(selamectin)

Vethical® Parasite Protection

Get protection from fleas, heartworm disease and intestinal parasites* in one monthly dose. Paradyne puts control in your hands, simply and effectively.

Produced for Dorling Kindersley by
Sands Publishing Solutions
4 Jenner Way, Eccles, Aylesford, Kent ME20 7SQ

Editorial Partners	David & Sylvia Tombesi-Walton
Design Partner	Simon Murrell
Project Editor	Chauney Dunford
Project Art Editor	Elaine Hewson
US Editor	Jill Hamilton
US Senior Editor	Shannon Beatty
Managing Editor	Penny Warren
Pre-production Producer	Heather Blagden
Producer	Rebecca Parton
Art Director	Jane Bull
Publisher	Mary Ling
Special Sales Creative Project Manager	Alison Donovan
Written by	Sylvia Tombesi-Walton
Consultant	Kim Bryan

This edition published in 2017
First American edition 2015
Published in the United States by DK Publishing
1450 Broadway, Suite 801, New York, NY 10018

Copyright © 2015, 2017 Dorling Kindersley Limited
DK, a Division of Penguin Random House LLC
19 20 21 22 10 9 8 7 6 5 4 3 2
003-307477-May/2017

A catalog record for this book is available from the Library of Congress.
ISBN 978-1-4654-8796-4

DK books are available at special discounts when purchased in bulk for sales
promotions, premiums, fund-raising, or educational use. For details, contact: DK Publishing
Special Markets, 1450 Broadway, Suite 801, New York, NY 10018 or SpecialSales@dk.com.

Printed and bound in China

A WORLD OF IDEAS:
SEE ALL THERE IS TO KNOW

www.dk.com

101 ESSENTIAL TIPS

Pages 8 to 15
DECIDING ON A CAT

1 ....Is a cat right for you?
2 ....Are you right for a cat?
3 ....Purebred or crossbreed?
4 ....Kitten or adult cat?
5 ....One cat or two?
6 ....Male or female?
7 ....Legal responsibilities
8 ....Indoor or outdoor cat?
9 ....Which breed? Playful cats
10 ....Which breed? Docile cats
11 ....Physical variations
12 ....Coats: long, short & special
13 ....Buying from breeders
14 ....Rescue shelters
15 ....Friends & acquaintances
16 ....Adopting a stray

Pages 16 to 29
YOUR NEW FRIEND

17 ....Cat-proof your home
18 ....Dangers in the home
19 ....Cat-proof your yard
20 ....Dangers in the yard
21 ....Baskets
22 ....Bedding

23 ....Feeding bowls
24 ....Litter box
25 ....Types of litter
26 ....Cat flap
27 ....Grooming equipment
28 ....Claw clippers
29 ....Carrying cases
30 ....Scratching posts
31 ....Toys
32 Checking the health of a new kitten
33 Checking the health of an adult cat
34 ....Settling in a new kitten
35 ....Settling in an adult cat
36 ....Choosing & teaching a name
37 ....Teaching a call sign
38 ....Microchipping
39 ....Vaccines
40 ....Neutering
41 ....Picking up a cat
42 ....Handling a cat
43 ....Meeting other cats & pets
44 ....Meeting children & friends

Pages 30 to 41
CARING FOR YOUR CAT

45	............................Wet & dry food
46	.................Provide enough water
47	.....................................Cat treats
48	...................................Giving milk
49	.............How much food & when?
50	...........................Setting a routine
51	...............................Where to feed
52	...................................Overfeeding
53	............Dealing with a fussy eater
54	........................Why cats eat grass
55	.........................Growing cat grass
56	............Grooming longhaired cats
57	...........Grooming shorthaired cats
58	........................Cleaning cats' eyes
59	........................Cleaning cats' ears
60	.....................Trimming cats' claws
61	..............Brushing your cat's teeth
62	...........................Bathing your cat
63	...............................Litter training
64	...........................Cat-flap training

Pages 42 to 47
LEARNING THE HOUSE RULES

65	...................Preventing scratching
66	...................Defining no-go areas
67	...................Dealing with straying
68	...........Rewarding good behavior
69	..................Combating aggression
70	...................Dealing with begging
71	............Looking for a missing cat
72	....Spraying
73	........................In or out at night?
74	.........................First time outside
75	.....................The hunting instinct
76	.......................Unwanted presents

Pages 48 to 53
LIVING WITH A CAT

77	..Reading negative body language
78	...Reading positive body language
79	................................Toys & play
80	.................Living with a timid cat
81	....Moving
82	......................Traveling with a cat
83	.........................Kennels & sitters

Pages 54 to 69
YOUR CAT'S HEALTH

84	....................Signs of good health
85	.............Caring for an elderly cat
86	............Caring for a pregnant cat
87	Controlling fleas, ticks & worms
88	................Dealing with hair balls
89	............Spotting signs of distress
90	....Wounds
91	....Stings
92	....Bites
93	.................When to go to the vet
94	................Symptoms of ill health
95	.................Common cat illnesses
96	..............Giving pills & medicine
97	.........................Giving eye drops
98	.........................Giving ear drops
99	...................Caring for a sick cat
100	........................Feeding a sick cat
101	...................Human health issues

Index 70

Acknowledgments 72

DECIDING ON A CAT

1 IS A CAT RIGHT FOR YOU?

Mysterious and entertaining, cats have a reputation for being independent, but they still rely on us for a range of needs. These include food, shelter, and veterinary care, but also affection and physical and mental stimulation. Cats will adapt easily to living indoors, but it is important to keep them entertained or they may get bored and develop bad habits such as scratching furniture or chewing plants.

PLAYING TOGETHER
Cats learn how to interact with other cats and with people during the first few weeks of their lives. This early socialization period is extremely important.

2 ARE YOU RIGHT FOR A CAT?

Before welcoming a cat into your home, be aware that costs—food, veterinary expenses, pet insurance, boarding when you go away —will add up. Consider your lifestyle, too: do you have the time and space to offer a suitably stimulating environment that caters to all of your cat's needs?

A LIFETIME OF LOVE
That kitten in your hands might live 15 years or more. You are responsible for its well-being.

3 PUREBRED OR CROSSBREED?

If you want to enter the world of cat shows, buy a purebred cat from a reputable breeder. Purebred cats are expensive, but by opting for a specific breed, you can expect certain physical and behavioral characteristics. If all you want is a low-maintenance companion, then a crossbreed shorthaired cat is probably your best option.

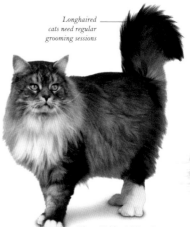

Longhaired cats need regular grooming sessions

Silver Tabby Maine Coon

Crossbreed with tabby markings

4 KITTEN OR ADULT CAT?

It can be easier to introduce a kitten than an adult cat into your home, especially if you already have a pet. However, adult cats tend to be less demanding and do not usually require any training. In addition, an adult cat is likely to have already been neutered, reducing the initial costs.

Kittens have more fun when they have playmates

Adult cat comes with fully developed personality

Inquisitive kittens

Young adult cat

5 ONE CAT OR TWO?

Two cats cost more than one, of course, but if you go out to work during the day, two cats can keep each other company, if you have room. Be sure to neuter cats of the opposite sex that live together, to avoid unwanted kittens. Also, an adult cat that is used to living alone might not welcome a feline companion.

LONELY & BORED
A cat left on its own for long periods of time can become bored and disruptive.

FRIENDS FOREVER
Bonded kittens will remain best friends for life. They will enjoy each other's company during playtime and often cuddle up together to sleep.

6 MALE OR FEMALE?

In general, female cats are more affectionate and playful than male cats, who are more likely to show territorial aggression. However, it should be personality, rather than gender, that dictates your choice of a cat. This is especially true after spaying or neutering, when any character differences between males and females tend to become less evident.

Cats of opposite sex often get along best

Adult male cats are often solitary creatures

Bonded male and female cats

7 LEGAL RESPONSIBILITIES

In some areas, cats are considered to have a right to roam; however, many localities have laws that protect homeowners from damage by neighbor's cats. Furthermore, before you allow your cat outside, you should consider your pet's effect on local bird populations: cats are predators and decimate populations of ground-nesting birds even if they are pets and well fed by their human owners.

YOUR RESPONSIBILITY TOWARD YOUR CAT

Under local and federal animal protection laws, cat owners have a duty of care toward their pet and are responsible for its welfare. This includes, among other things, a proper diet, a suitable environment, the opportunity to exhibit normal behavior, and protection from pain, suffering, and injury.

8 INDOOR OR OUTDOOR CAT?

Cats do enjoy exploring the great outdoors, but they face many dangers there. These include speeding vehicles, parasites and infectious diseases, predators, and even other cats. Indoor cats are healthier and live longer than their outdoor friends but require regular play sessions. You can give your cat the outdoor experience without the dangers by constructing a cat run.

ARMCHAIR HUNTER
Make sure you give your indoor cat access to a window. It will enjoy spending time looking at the outside world from the safety of its home environment.

KING OF THE YARD
Before you let your cat roam outdoors, make sure it is safe for it to do so. If your yard is already part of another cat's territory, you may need to accompany your cat out at first.

11

9 WHICH BREED? PLAYFUL CATS

Through playing, kittens learn the skills they need to interact socially and to hunt. Some cats carry their love of playtime into adulthood. Particularly energetic cat breeds include Abyssinians, Devon or Cornish Rexes, and Siamese. Neutering your cat before it reaches sexual maturity ensures that it will remain playful into its adult life.

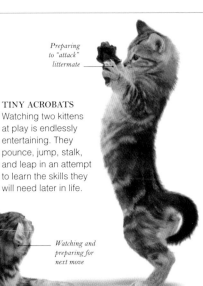

Preparing to "attack" littermate

TINY ACROBATS
Watching two kittens at play is endlessly entertaining. They pounce, jump, stalk, and leap in an attempt to learn the skills they will need later in life.

Watching and preparing for next move

10 WHICH BREED? DOCILE CATS

If the idea of having regular playful sessions with your cat does not appeal to you, you could opt for a breed with a low level of playfulness. Some breeds—including Ragdolls, Persians (or Longhairs), and British Shorthairs—are especially docile and laid-back. The Ragdoll, in particular, is famous for its tendency to relax completely and go limp in the arms of a trusted person. If you want to keep your cat indoors, it might be best to choose one of these breeds.

CHILLING OUT
Ragdoll cats such as this one enjoy a relaxing environment.

11 PHYSICAL VARIATIONS

There are many cat breeds, each with a different set of physical characteristics. While some of these attributes have evolved naturally, others have come about as a result of selective breeding. Variations include coat length and color, body shape, and eye shape and color.

FACE & EYES
Cats' faces can be wedge-shaped or round; their eyes can range in color from orange and amber, to green and blue.

BODY SHAPE
Cats' body shapes have evolved to suit the climate in their places of origin. Stocky breeds usually hail from cold countries, while lithe breeds often originate from countries with a warm climate.

Muscular

Slim

Stocky

12 COATS: LONG, SHORT & SPECIAL

Cats are loosely divided into two groups: longhaired and shorthaired. However, some breeds do not fall into either camp, such as the hairless Sphynx and the various Rex breeds, with their wavy, rippled hair. All cats produce proteins in their saliva, skin, and urine that are transferred to their coats and can cause reactions in some people; if you or someone in your home is so afflicted, consider one of the so-called hypoallergenic breeds.

LONG COAT
A longhaired cat's coat needs daily brushing and regular grooming, or it will become matted.

SHORT COAT
Shorthaired cats tend to groom themselves, but you can help them with regular brushing.

HAIRLESS
Although known as a hairless cat, the Sphynx is actually covered with a layer of fine down.

REX COAT
Devon, Cornish, and Selkirk Rex cats have a wavy coat that is silky and soft to the touch.

13

13 BUYING FROM BREEDERS

If you have done your research and know which breed you want, the next thing to do is contact a specialist breeder. This is particularly important if you want to show your cat or to breed from it. A reliable breeder will be able to identify potential winners within a litter. When you buy a purebred kitten from a breeder, ask if you may see its mother, too. Good breeders will always be happy to oblige.

SIBERIAN FOREST
These Siberian Forest kittens are still too young to leave their mother. A good breeder will wait until the kittens are at least 12 weeks old before releasing them.

Cat cage at a rescue shelter

14 RESCUE SHELTERS

Cat shelters are full to bursting with abandoned cats and kittens in need of loving homes. If you are looking for a feline companion rather than a show cat, consider adopting from a shelter. Any adult cats will have been neutered already, reducing your initial expense. You may be asked for a donation toward the running of the shelter.

15 FRIENDS & ACQUAINTANCES

Another way of obtaining a cat is by spreading the word among your friends and family. Somebody might know someone else whose cat has just had a litter and who is hoping to have the kittens adopted into good homes. Your veterinary clinic is another good source of information.

Littermates cozying up together

ADOPTING A STRAY

16 If a stray-looking cat keeps visiting your yard and you want to give it a home, start by leaving some food out for it. If it is approachable, take the cat to the vet to establish whether it is indeed a stray. The vet will be able to check if the cat is microchipped and simply lost. If the cat is a stray, have it examined for infectious diseases and vaccinated, and find out if it has been neutered, before taking it into your home. This is especially important if you already have cats.

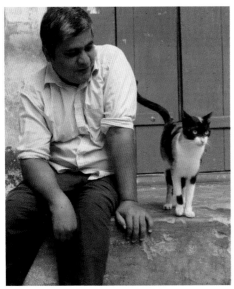

GENTLY, GENTLY
Slowly approach cats that seem to be strays—they may be fearful of people and react by scratching or hissing. Better yet, sit and let them come to you in their own time.

STRAY OR FERAL?
While stray cats are often abandoned or lost ones that have lived with a human family for some time, feral cats have had no significant interaction with humans. They are often nervous and unapproachable.

GAINING TRUST
Leave some food out for the stray cat. At the start, it might not eat until after you have left, but it will soon come to think of you as a provider of food. Move the bowl a little closer to your door each day.

YOUR NEW FRIEND

17 CAT-PROOF YOUR HOME

Before you bring your new cat to live with you, make sure that your home provides a safe environment for it. Cats are curious by nature, so invest in a few childproof latches to prevent them from exploring food cabinets, china cabinets, and garbage and trash cans. It is also wise to purchase some safety covers for any electrical outlets.

Make sure windows are closed or on a latch to prevent accidental falls

Keep door of washing machine closed at all times

Put cat's litter box in an out-of-the-way corner

Make sure cat's food station is in a quiet area

18 DANGERS IN THE HOME

Some substances routinely found in the home are toxic for cats and could be potentially fatal if ingested. These range from household cleaning products and antifreeze, to human painkillers and some decorative house plants and flowers, such as poinsettia, mistletoe, and lilies. Long cords from curtains and blinds may also be hazardous for inquisitive cats, as can needles, thread, and rubber bands.

19 CAT-PROOF YOUR YARD

Wait until your cat is familiar with and comfortable in its new home before allowing it to go outside. This could take a couple of weeks. Use this time to cat-proof your yard. Make sure there are no holes or gaps in the fences; while most cats will be able to climb over, a fence should prevent dogs, foxes, and other predators from coming into your yard.

20 DANGERS IN THE YARD

The dangers in the yard are similar to those in the home—that is, toxic substances such as weedkillers, pesticides, and slug and snail pellets. Close every container carefully, and store it in a cat-proof shed. Also use the shed to store sharp and heavy gardening tools. Other hazards include toxic plants such as ivy, rhododendron, and clematis.

Lid on stove prevents accidents

Cat flap allows cat to let itself in and out of house

Cats enjoy spending time in greenhouses and sheds, but make sure they can find a way out

Leave bowl full of water outside

Fence might help prevent encounters with other animals

Make sure plants in your yard are not toxic for your cat

21 BASKETS

Cats spend most of the day sleeping or napping, so make sure their sleeping quarters are cozy, comfortable, and in a quiet area of the house. Cats enjoy feeling snug and warm, so consider buying a basket with high, padded sides and a cushioned center that, ideally, is removable and washable.

Igloo cat bed

BASKET CHOICES
There are many types of cat baskets on the market—from igloos, to wicker and padded varieties.

Cat basket

Plush basket

Kitten snoozing on fleece bedding

22 BEDDING

Choose bedding material that is comfortable, soft, and machine-washable. Cats love being warm, so for the winter months, consider buying a fleecy bed that hangs from the radiator, allowing your cat to be as close to a heat source as possible. If your radiators are not suitable for this type of bed, a self-warming bed is the next best thing. Many cats enjoy nothing better than sleeping on a blanket on your lap.

23 FEEDING BOWLS

Cats are fussy eaters with an extremely well-developed sense of smell. Keep their eating station clean and wash their feeding bowls at least daily, especially in the warm summer months. Feeding bowls come in a range of materials—from plastic and metal, to ceramic. If buying a plastic or metal bowl, make sure it has rubber feet to prevent it from sliding around the floor.

Plastic bowl

Metal bowl

24 LITTER BOX

There are two types of litter box: open and covered. Choose your favorite and stick with it, because a cat that is used to an open box may feel nervous about switching to a covered one, and vice versa. Place the box in a quiet corner, well away from your cat's feeding station. Scoop out any stools and clumps of urine several times a day to keep the tray as clean as possible.

Poop scoop

25 TYPES OF LITTER

There are many types of litter available. As with the litter box, try to stick with whatever your cat has grown used to. Clumping litter is convenient in terms of scooping out feces and urine; however, what is appealing to us is not always acceptable to our cats—for example, perfumed litter often deters cats from using the litter box altogether.

Nonabsorbent litter   Fuller's earth litter   Lightweight litter   Wood-based litter

26 CAT FLAP

If your cat is an indoor/ outdoor cat, have a cat flap installed. They range from simple models that open inward and outward, to others that feature a locking dial. This allows you to leave the flap fully open, fully closed, or so that it opens only inward; this way, the cat can enter but not leave the house. The most sophisticated allow a cat through based on reading its microchip.

IN & OUT AS THEY PLEASE
A cat flap allows a cat the freedom to come and go, but the locking dial gives cat owners ultimate control.

Magnetic strip

Locking dial

27 GROOMING EQUIPMENT

Most cats enjoy being brushed. However, a regular brushing routine is vital for longhaired cats because it helps them maintain a glossy, snarl-free coat. The most important tools are a toothed comb, a slicker brush with soft wire bristles, and a soft brush. Accustom your cat to having its teeth brushed from an early age.

TOOLS OF THE TRADE
You will need combs and brushes, and a toothbrush.

EMERGENCY ALTERNATIVE
Cat claw clippers are the best and most accurate tool to use, but human clippers may be used with care if necessary.

28 CLAW CLIPPERS

Get your cat into the habit of having its claws trimmed regularly. This is especially important for indoor cats, which are less likely to wear down their claws. Press gently on each paw pad to expose the claw, then, using cat claw clippers, cut just the white tip of the nail. Do not cut to the quick; this will cause bleeding and may risk infection if not treated quickly.

Cat claw clippers

29 CAT CARRIERS

Most cats do not take naturally to walking on a leash, so a cat carrier is essential. Carriers come in various materials: wicker, plastic, cardboard, or wire. Because you will mostly use a carrier for trips to the vet, your cat might associate it with bad experiences. Prevent this from happening by turning it into a safe place for your cat: leave it out at all times, maybe next to a radiator, and put a warm blanket in there.

Cat carrier

30 SCRATCHING POSTS

Cats scratch for a variety of reasons, not least marking their territory and keeping their claws sharp. To help prevent your cat from scratching destructively around the home, provide it with a scratching post. Some scratching posts double as multifunctional units, with sleeping areas, hanging toys, and other features.

Pyramidal scratching post

Dangling toys

Scratching post with platform

Scratching post

31 TOYS

It is important to keep your cat physically active and mentally stimulated. Provide a selection of toys to chase, swat, pounce on, and bite to re-create the feel and thrill of the hunt and keep your cat active, youthful, fit, and happy. Interacting with your cat at playtime will also strengthen the bond between you.

Plastic ball

Rolling toy

Fluffy toy

Catnip mouse

32 CHECKING THE HEALTH OF A NEW KITTEN

A healthy cat could be your companion for 15 years or more. If you are getting a kitten, choose carefully and spend some time with it observing its behavior before bringing it home. Consider the way it interacts with you and its siblings. Vitality and playfulness are important indicators of good health, as is an inquisitive attitude. There are also a few key checks to help establish the overall well-being of a kitten.

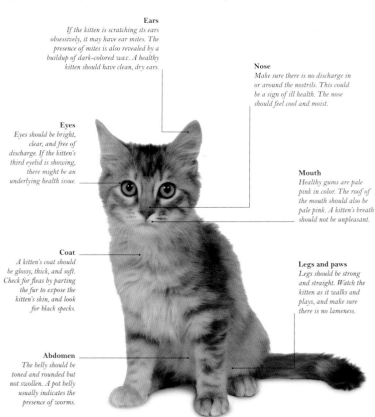

Ears
If the kitten is scratching its ears obsessively, it may have ear mites. The presence of mites is also revealed by a buildup of dark-colored wax. A healthy kitten should have clean, dry ears.

Nose
Make sure there is no discharge in or around the nostrils. This could be a sign of ill health. The nose should feel cool and moist.

Eyes
Eyes should be bright, clear, and free of discharge. If the kitten's third eyelid is showing, there might be an underlying health issue.

Mouth
Healthy gums are pale pink in color. The roof of the mouth should also be pale pink. A kitten's breath should not be unpleasant.

Coat
A kitten's coat should be glossy, thick, and soft. Check for fleas by parting the fur to expose the kitten's skin, and look for black specks.

Legs and paws
Legs should be strong and straight. Watch the kitten as it walks and plays, and make sure there is no lameness.

Abdomen
The belly should be toned and rounded but not swollen. A pot belly usually indicates the presence of worms.

33

CHECKING THE HEALTH OF AN ADULT CAT

It is a good idea to learn to recognize the indicators of feline ill health and to acclimatize your cat to regular home examinations. This will allow you to catch any potential problems at an early stage. Carry out a home examination when your cat is relaxed, perhaps while he is on your lap, and over the course of several days. Reward your cat's cooperation with a treat or a cuddle. If anything appears wrong, take your cat to the vet. Outdoor cats should be checked more often than indoor ones.

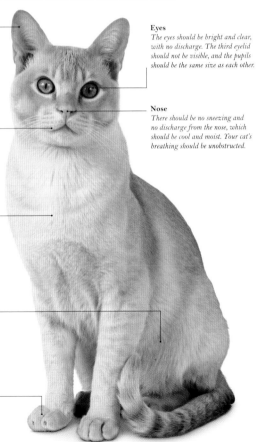

Ears
An adult cat's ears should be clean, dry, and free of unpleasant odors. If your cat holds its head to the side or shakes it and scratches its ears, there may be an infection or mites present.

Eyes
The eyes should be bright and clear, with no discharge. The third eyelid should not be visible, and the pupils should be the same size as each other.

Nose
There should be no sneezing and no discharge from the nose, which should be cool and moist. Your cat's breathing should be unobstructed.

Mouth
Your cat's gums should be pale pink, its teeth white and strong, and its breath not unpleasant. A buildup of tartar and inflamed gums might mean that you have to improve its oral hygiene.

Coat
A cat's coat is a great indicator of good health. It should be glossy and thick; if it sits up in patches or becomes dull, take your cat to the vet. Also look for bald patches, scratches, excessive shedding, and parasites.

Abdomen
Run your hands down the side of your cat. You should be able to feel an indent at its waist. If your cat's stomach is round and protruding, it might be overweight or pregnant.

Paws
Your cat should distribute its weight through all four legs and show no signs of discomfort when it walks or jumps.

Your New Friend

34 SETTLING IN A NEW KITTEN

Bring your kitten home at a time when you can spend a couple of days bonding with it. Bear in mind that it will be away from its mother and littermates for the first time in its life, so create an environment in which it will feel calm and secure. For the first few days, do little beside sitting in the room with it, ideally at floor level, so the kitten can investigate and get to know you.

1 Place the carrier in a quiet room and open the door. The kitten will probably observe its surroundings from the safety of the carrier.

2 Give the kitten time to build up its confidence. It will come out of the carrier in its own time and start exploring the room.

Children can help, but they should to be supervised

CHILDREN & KITTENS

Your children will be excited about the new arrival. Allow them to help settle the kitten in, but make sure they maintain a calm, quiet demeanor.

Kitten is attracted to food

SETTLING IN AN ADULT CAT

35

Coming from a rescue shelter or another family, an adult cat might find settling into your home as stressful as a kitten would. The same approach applies: do not force the cat out of the carrier, but let it come out in its own time and allow it to explore just one room at the start. Create a calm environment, with a couple of places for the cat to hide should it feel threatened or nervous. Get to know each other.

INITIATING CONTACT
Let the cat explore its surroundings without interference. Allow it to initiate contact with you, which it will do when it feels confident.

Big pupils in bright light indicate fear

Walking low to the floor

FEARFUL BEGINNINGS
In new, unfamiliar surroundings, a cat might display fearful behavior, such as hiding under the bed, crouching low to the floor, or walking close to the walls. Do not add to its fear by trying to approach it. Give it time.

36 CHOOSING & TEACHING A NAME

If you bought your cat from a breeder, it will have a registered pedigree name, which is often quite a mouthful. In everyday life, your cat's name should be one or two syllables at most, such as Homie, Rudy, Lyra, or Zack. To teach your cat its name, repeat it as you give treats. A cat adopted from a rescue shelter may already have a name, and staff there may advise you to keep it.

POPULAR NAMES

As T. S. Eliot suggested in his poem on the subject, it is no easy task to name your feline friend. You might want to get to know your cat a little before giving it the name that will accompany it for the rest of its life.

A cat's name may be inspired by a particularly strong personality trait or by a physical characteristic—a white cat may be named Snowy, for example; a black one, Sooty; and a cat with only half a tail might be Stumpy.

Some people choose to name their cats after their favorite actor, or other personality.

SHORT ATTENTION SPAN
Kittens are hard to train because they are easily distracted.

37 TEACHING A CALL SIGN

Training sessions with cats should last just a few minutes and ideally take place before mealtimes. Say, "Come!" and shake a package of your cat's favorite treats. When it comes, give it a treat. Move away and repeat this exercise a couple of times. Cats respond to positive reinforcement and will soon learn to come to the call sign even without the rattling sound of the snack package.

REWARD TRAINING
Cats are very intelligent and trainable creatures. The secret is to find a reward they enjoy and that keeps them motivated to learn, whether it be a food treat or a cuddle.

38 MICROCHIPPING

The most reliable way of identifying a lost cat and having it reunited with its family is by microchipping it. Unlike collars and tags, which can come undone, the microchip is permanently embedded under the cat's skin. A microchip is about the size of a grain of rice. Each has a unique code that is linked to the contact details of the cat's owner in a database.

INSERTING THE MICROCHIP
The microchip is inserted in the back of a cat's neck by means of an injection. The cat will have no awareness of it.

SCANNING FOR A MICROCHIP
When a stray cat is taken to a vet or a rescue shelter, it is routinely scanned for a microchip to see if it has a family.

39 VACCINES

Have your kitten vaccinated against three potentially fatal viruses: feline infectious enteritis, feline influenza, and feline leukemia. You are advised to do this even if your cat is indoor only. You may have to use a kennel one day, and vaccinations are mandatory for residents. If you are acquiring an adult cat from a shelter, confirm that its vaccinations are up to date.

KITTEN'S FIRST VACCINATION
Kittens are usually vaccinated at between eight and ten weeks. Throughout its life, a cat will also require annual boosters.

40 NEUTERING

Unless you have a pedigree cat that you want to breed, it is wise to neuter your cat. Male cats should be castrated at about four months to prevent undesirable behavior such as roaming, fighting, and spraying. Female cats can be spayed as early as four months to avoid unwanted pregnancies. Neutering is a routine operation that is carried out under anesthetic.

41 PICKING UP A CAT

You may need to gain the trust of an adult cat before you can pick it up. Let it come to you and sniff you; then pet it gently. Put one hand under the cat's chest, and support its hind legs with the other. Lift it up slowly, all the time holding it close to your chest so it feels secure.

Relaxed cat

KNOW WHEN TO PICK UP
Be mindful of cat body language. Once you have your hand under its chest, only proceed to pick up the cat if it remains calm.

42 HANDLING A CAT

After you have picked up your cat, cradle it gently against your chest. Create as many points of contact as you can between your body and your cat's. This will increase its feeling of safety. If a cat starts struggling while in your arms, put it back down as quickly and gently as you can. Try to maintain a hold on the cat without getting scratched until it is safely on the ground.

FEELING SNUG
With firm support around and under its hindquarters, this cat looks relaxed in the arms of its owner. Stroking the cat while holding it also reassures it.

Inquisitive, alert look

43 MEETING OTHER CATS & PETS

Keep the new cat and the established pet in separate rooms at first, switching them around every few days, so they can become familiar with each other's smell. Supervise the first few meetings, making sure the new arrival has a safe place to retreat to in the event of an aggressive reaction.

Curious dog

Apprehensive kitten

CAT MEETS DOG
Contrary to popular belief, cats and dogs can become good friends, especially when introduced to each other at a young age.

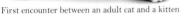
First encounter between an adult cat and a kitten

44 MEETING CHILDREN & FRIENDS

Children can often be too loud and boisterous for cats and kittens, so supervise early encounters until you are confident that both are comfortable in each other's presence. As ever, allow the cat to make the first move, and do not force it to be in the presence of any houseguests.

SITTING PRETTY
The safest approach with young children is to have them sit on the floor with a cushion on their lap. Gently place the kitten on the cushion.

CAREFUL HANDLING
Make sure children pick up and handle the cat in the correct manner.

29

CARING FOR YOUR CAT

45 WET & DRY FOOD

Commercial cat food is scientifically formulated to provide your cat with a balanced diet that meets all of its nutritional needs. Kittens and senior cats, which have slightly different dietary requirements from adult cats, have their own ranges of food. To add variety to your cat's diet, buy wet food in a range of flavors and supply it in conjunction with dry food and fresh food. Introduce any dietary changes slowly to avoid stomach upsets.

DRY FOOD
These come in various flavors and are good for keeping your cat's teeth free of tartar.

Boneless fish flakes

Minced chicken and turkey

Tuna chunks

Lamb chunks

DRY FOOD
This cat appears to have a preference for dry food. Some dried foods are especially suited to specific dietary needs—for example, dealing with hair ball relief or weight control.

WET FOOD
A stunningly diverse range of flavors—from fish, to poultry, to meat—ensures that no cat ever has to grow bored with the food in its bowl.

PROVIDE ENOUGH WATER

Cats are desert animals with a relatively low thirst drive, and they draw most of the water they need from the food they consume. However, it is important to provide your cat with a bowl of fresh water at all times, especially if it has a predilection for dry food, which has a very low moisture content. Some cats prefer to drink running water, and they might make a beeline for a faucet if it is turned on.

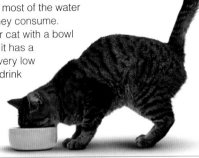

Drinking water from a bowl

CAT TREATS

There are many types of cat treats on the market, so choose wisely. Avoid treats with a high fat content, and instead opt for those that are high in protein, such as dried fish flakes. Treats can also help keep teeth and gums healthy. The key word with treats is moderation.

TREAT RAINBOW
Like wet and dry food, cat treats come in a wide range of flavors, as well as different shapes and textures.

Drinking special kitten milk

GIVING MILK

One of the most persistent feline myths is that cats love a saucer of milk. However, not only is milk not essential to a cat's diet, but many cats are actually lactose-intolerant, so drinking cow's milk can lead to a stomach upset. The only exception concerns young kittens, who need their mother's milk to grow up and thrive. If the mother is not around or not producing enough milk, you will have to feed the kitten a special formula, which may be partly cow's milk.

31

49 HOW MUCH FOOD & WHEN?

Cats are obligate carnivores, which means they need meat to survive. Unlike dogs, cats are not usually greedy, and they will adjust their calorie intake to their level of activity. As a result, as a cat grows older and less active, it might start to eat less. If you are concerned, ask your vet for advice on an older cat's food intake.

MULTIPLE BOWLS
In order to prevent competitive eating, it is advisable to give each cat in your household its own feeding bowl.

FEEDING GUIDE
This chart is an estimate of daily feeding requirements (in calories, as well as number of ounces of both wet and dry food) of your cat, based on its current weight and lifestyle.

Adult weight	4½ lb	9 lb	13 lb	22 lb	26½ lb
Inactive cat	100–140 cal (4¼ oz wet/ 1 oz dry)	200–280 cal (8½ oz wet/ 2 oz dry)	300–420 cal (12⅜ oz wet/ 3¼ oz dry)	400–560 cal (17 oz wet/ 4¼ oz dry)	500–700 cal (21⅛ oz wet/ 5¼ oz dry)
Active cat	140–180 cal (5½ oz wet/ 1⅓ oz dry)	280–360 cal (11¼ oz wet/ 2¾ oz dry)	420–540 cal (17 oz wet/ 4¼ oz dry)	560–720 cal (22½ oz wet/ 5½ oz dry)	700–900 cal (28⅛ oz wet/ 7 oz dry)
Pregnant female	200–280 cal (8½ oz wet/ 2 oz dry)	400–560 cal (17 oz wet/ 4¼ oz dry)	600–840 cal (25½ oz wet/ 6¼ oz dry)	800–1,120 cal (33⅜ oz wet/ 8½ oz dry)	1,000–1,400 cal (42¼ oz wet/ 10½ oz dry)

50 SETTING A ROUTINE

Some people work long hours outside the home and resort to free-feeding their cats. This means the cat has food at its disposal and can eat when it is hungry. In such cases, use dry food, which doesn't go bad in the heat. However, if your lifestyle allows it, opt to establish a feeding routine for your cat. Feed it two meals a day, at regular times, but leave a bowl of water out at all times.

Enjoying a meal at dinner time

51 WHERE TO FEED

Create a feeding corner in an out-of-the-way area of the kitchen without much foot traffic. Cats have a very keen sense of smell, so keep their eating area clean. If you have a multiple-cat household, give each cat its own bowl. This will prevent squabbles over food and make it easier for you to track each cat's eating habits.

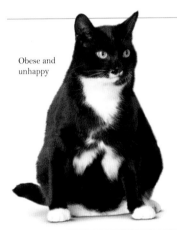

Obese and unhappy

52 OVERFEEDING

Be careful not to overfeed your cat, especially if it is an indoor cat without many opportunities to burn calories. Overfeeding could lead to obesity, which brings with it a host of health issues, ranging from difficulty grooming and joint problems, to potentially life-threatening conditions such as diabetes and heart disorders. If you are not overfeeding your cat but it is still putting on weight, it could be due to a hormonal imbalance. Consult your vet.

53 DEALING WITH A FUSSY EATER

If your cat becomes a fussy eater, try feeding it a different flavor or a different brand of wet food. Keep a list of the flavors it likes. Consider the cleanliness of the feeding station. Remove any scraps of old food and wash the bowl before refilling it. If your cat still will not eat, there may be an underlying health issue. Talk to your vet.

SNIFFING FROM AFAR
Feed your cat strong-smelling food to attract it to its bowl.

54 WHY CATS EAT GRASS

Although grass has no real nutritional value, it plays an important role in your cat's diet. Cats eat grass because it facilitates the bringing up of indigestible matter sitting in your cat's stomach, such as hair balls. If your cat has no access to a lawn, you should provide it with some indoor greenery. Beware, though: some plants may be toxic to your cat. Stick with special kitty grass or opt for cat-friendly herbs like thyme, sage, or parsley.

Munching on grass

CREATE A KITTY LAWN
You may not have a lawn, but it is easy to grow some cat-friendly grass in a pot. Your cat will nibble as it feels the need—and thank you by bringing up a hair ball!

55 GROWING CAT GRASS

Grow-your-own-grass kits can be found in most pet stores and well-stocked supermarkets. Just follow the simple directions on the package, and within a week you should have a miniature grassy lawn for your cat. The grass in these containers keeps well for up to three weeks. Alternatively, devote a patch of your garden to plants that your cat might enjoy (see Tip 54).

Thick, luscious grass

Foil container

Grow-your-own-grass kit

56 GROOMING LONGHAIRED CATS

Longhaired cats need a helping hand with grooming. Daily brushing sessions prevent the formation of painful snarls and mats in the fur and help remove loose hairs. Without brushing, these hairs would be ingested by your cat, leading to large hair balls in its stomach and subsequent regurgitation. A good bonding exercise, grooming is also beneficial to the cat's circulation and helps distribute natural oils all over its coat, which helps keep it in good condition. Another advantage is that the regular handling of your cat allows you to become aware of any abnormalities or lumps on its body.

1 Brush your cat when it is feeling calm and relaxed. Start by running a slicker brush all down its back and sides. Be gentle, and do not pull —there might be snarls in the fur that need to be untangled.

2 Next, using a metal comb, work through the cat's fur, loosening any mats and snarls. Comb both toward the tail and toward the head. Working toward the head allows you to check your cat's skin for parasites and injuries.

3 The belly and the legs are very sensitive. If there are snarls, loosen them with your fingers rather than the metal comb. Finish on the tail with a wide-toothed comb or brush.

57 GROOMING SHORTHAIRED CATS

Although shorthaired cats do not require the same level of brushing as longhaired cats, it is advisable to establish a weekly grooming routine to keep their coats glossy and in good condition. Regular handling also allows you to spot any abnormalities that might otherwise go unnoticed. Operate in a calm, relaxed environment, and watch out for any signs of nervousness or discomfort from your cat during the session.

CHILD'S PLAY
Brushing a shorthaired cat is considerably easier than brushing a longhair. At its simplest, it is just a matter of running a brush gently down its coat to remove loose hairs.

1 Start by working a slicker brush down the back and sides of your cat. If it allows you, brush its abdomen, too. Be gentle, though, since this is a very sensitive area.

2 Using a metal comb, part the fur to check for fleas, scratches, and other injuries. If you like, apply a few drops of coat conditioner to enhance the shine of your cat's coat.

REGULAR STROKING

Some cats do not enjoy being brushed and combed. However, even regular stroking goes some way toward ensuring that your pet maintains a healthy, glossy coat.

In addition, there are benefits for us, too, because stroking a cat has been shown to lower blood pressure and relieve stress.

58 CLEANING CATS' EYES

Some cats, especially longhaired cats with shortened faces—Persians (or Longhairs) and Himalayans, for example—need a little help to keep their eyes clean. This is because their tear ducts are particularly prone to blocking up, leading to a buildup of gunk. If left for even just a day, this discharge can turn crusty, which makes it even harder to remove. Eventually, it can even lead to an unsightly discoloration of the fur around the eyes and nose. If you notice an unusual crusty buildup around your cat's eyes, there may be an underlying health issue, so speak to your vet.

REGULAR INSPECTION

A regular examination of your cat's eyes helps catch problems at an early stage. A visible third eyelid is a sign of ill health or injury; the latter is more likely if only one eye is affected. If your cat keeps an eye closed, it might have been scratched or have a foreign body in it.

1 Dampen a piece of cotton with lukewarm water or, if the buildup seems particularly stubborn, with a saline solution such as you would use for contact lenses. Wipe from the nose toward the temple.

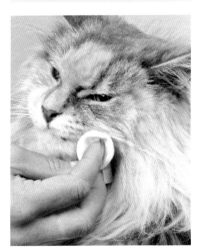

2 Repeat the process on the other eye with a clean piece of cotton. If your cat allows it, try to remove any staining on its fur, too. Avoid your cat's eyeball during cleaning because is it could lead to irritation.

Caring for Your Cat

59 CLEANING CATS' EARS

Although cats are perfectly capable of looking after their ears, a regular cleaning routine has the added benefit of allowing you to keep an eye out for parasites, scratches, and other issues (see right). Outdoor cats, for example, might come home with barbed seeds or spiky grass stuck inside their ears. Foreign bodies should be removed from your cat's ears only if they are on the surface. Anything lodged in the ear canal should be removed by the vet. To clean your cat's ears, you will need some cotton and a few drops of baby oil.

REGULAR INSPECTION
Black spots, dark wax, or redness indicate the presence of ear mites. If you see a liquid discharge, consult your vet. Also look for scratches and bald patches. If your cat has white ears, make sure there are no scabs and sores around the tips of its ears, since this could be a sign of skin cancer.

1 Hold your cat's head gently but firmly, and fold back its ear. Using a piece of cotton moistened with a few drops of baby oil, wipe away any dirt that you can see on the inside of the ear.

2 Cats have very sensitive ears, so be gentle. Do not rub, but rather try to lift any waxy buildup onto the cotton. Never use a cotton swab, which could cause serious damage to the ear canal.

TRIMMING CATS' CLAWS

60

Outdoor cats usually wear down their claws by walking on paved areas and scratching trees and wooden posts. However, indoor cats need to have their claws trimmed regularly, to prevent them from growing so long that they inhibit normal movement or pierce the paw pad. Claws are important parts of your cat's anatomy. Never consider declawing your cat just to solve a scratching problem. Declawing involves the removal of the last joint of a cat's toe. It is a cruel and painful procedure.

Apply pressure on paw pad

Exposed claw

How to expose the claw

1 Unless your cat is very calm, cut just a couple of claws per session. Holding your cat still, apply a little pressure on its paw pad to reveal the claw to trim.

Hard cuticle

Quick

Cutting line

Cat claw anatomy

2 Using clippers, cut just the white tip of the claw. Be careful not to cut too close to the pink quick. It is better to cut too little than too much, especially if your cat is struggling to get free from your hold.

61 BRUSHING YOUR CAT'S TEETH

The most important thing about brushing a cat's teeth is not to use human toothpaste. Buy a pet-specific product. Before progressing to a toothbrush, try a little toothpaste on the cat's lips, then touch a cotton swab to its gums. You will probably need to hold the cat firmly but gently.

THIMBLE BRUSH
Thimble-style toothbrushes are available for pets. These slip over the end of your finger for improved maneuverability in cleaning.

62 BATHING YOUR CAT

Most cats do not enjoy being bathed, but sometimes it is necessary, especially with longhaired cats, which have the hardest time grooming themselves. However, don't try to remove any substance that is not water soluble—oil, for example—without first consulting a vet. Before you start, gather your equipment, and consider asking a friend to help hold the cat. Talk soothingly to the cat throughout to keep it as calm as possible.

1 Place your cat in a bowl with about 4 in (10 cm) of warm water. Use a showerhead or a pitcher to pour warm water over the cat.

2 When the cat's coat is fully soaked, apply a small amount of cat shampoo. Avoid the cat's face, especially its eyes and ears.

3 Massage the shampoo deep into your cat's coat, all the way down its body. Rinse well, with lots of warm water.

4 Wrap the cat in a towel and pat it dry. You may need to use a hair dryer on a quiet, low setting for longhaired cats.

63

LITTER TRAINING

Most cats will take to the litter box with little difficulty. Litter training requires mostly just good timing on your part. Wait until the kitten looks like it is ready to use the litter box—it will raise its tail as it crouches down—and place it in the tray. Instinct will usually do the rest: the kitten will cover its feces, and the smell will guide it to the tray whenever the need arises.

EARLY LEARNING
Reward a kitten with praise or a treat when it uses the litter box. This will encourage repeated use.

Litter-box liner

CLEAN LITTER
Cats are fastidious animals. Scoop the litter box regularly to keep it clean and odor-free.

64

CAT FLAP TRAINING

If your cat is going to be an indoor/outdoor cat, you will need to install a cat flap and train your cat how to use it. The flap should be installed at about 6 in (15 cm) from the floor for the cat to be able to use it comfortably. Prop it open at first, and encourage your cat to come through with a toy or a food treat. When your cat is confident using the hole, close the flap and repeat the training process, this time, teaching your cat to push the flap open with its paw or head.

FOOD LURE
A bowl full of your cat's favorite food should be incentive enough for it to come through the cat flap.

LEARNING THE HOUSE RULES

65 PREVENTING SCRATCHING

Cats have scent glands in their paws, and in nature they use scratching as a way of marking their territory. However, in the home, this natural instinct can turn into undesirable behavior when cats scratch furniture and curtains. Prevent this from happening by channeling your cat's desire to scratch toward a well-positioned scratching post. Keeping your cat's claws trimmed also helps.

NIP IT IN THE BUD
If your cat is clawing at a table leg or sofa, cover the part of the furniture that your cat wants to scratch with plastic, then place a scratching post next to it.

Scratching post

66 DEFINING NO-GO AREAS

To enjoy a peaceful cohabitation with your cat, you might need to impose limits on where it is allowed. Although some cats like to sleep with their human family, this could end up disrupting your own sleeping pattern. Keep the door to your bedroom closed, and put your cat's bed in another quiet area of the house.

NO ACCESS
Close your bedroom door if you do not want your cat to enter. The door should be closed at all times, not just at night.

Cats love a cozy human bed

67 DEALING WITH STRAYING

The main step to prevent your cat from straying is having it neutered. This will help curb its territorial roaming instincts. In addition, be sure to provide your cat with a safe and inviting home environment that it will want to return to again and again. Make sure it has enough food and plenty of mental and physical stimulation. Finally, keep your cat indoors after dark.

Tail held high   *Determined gait*

QUIET TIME
A chaotic household might lead a cat to seek peace and solitude elsewhere. Create a quiet area for your cat within the house.

FOOD-SEEKING MISSION
Some straying behavior is related to the need for food. Make sure you give your cat enough to eat.

68 REWARDING GOOD BEHAVIOR

Cats respond better to rewards than discipline. Rather than reprimanding your cat for unwanted behavior like scratching the sofa, give it a cuddle or a food treat every time it uses the scratching post. Be sure to provide the reward right after the cat displays good behavior, so it will associate the two.

FAVORITE TREAT
Some cats enjoy food treats. For others, soothing words, a stroke or a vigorous play session are better rewards.

69 COMBATING AGGRESSION

It is unusual for cats to behave aggressively toward people. When this happens, it is important to understand the reasons behind it. First of all, take your cat to the vet to rule out ill health. Cats become aggressive when they feel threatened, but some may do so when they are bored, so try to create a stimulating environment for your cat.

Ears folded down

TOWARD PEOPLE
Pain, fear, and frustration are all potential causes of feline aggression. Understanding the reason is the key to providing a solution.

TOWARD OTHER CATS
If your cat behaves aggressively toward another cat, it could be due to sharing territory or other resources, such as food.

70 DEALING WITH BEGGING

Cats are unlikely to beg for table scraps the way dogs would. However, when this happens, it is important to put a stop to it before the begging turns into jumping on the table at dinner time. Feeding your cat before sitting down for your own dinner will make it less likely to beg for food. If this fails, shut your cat in a different room while you eat.

Scavenging through garbage

MANIPULATIVE CAT
Giving in to your cat when it is begging opens the door for more undesirable behavior.

71 LOOKING FOR A MISSING CAT

Always on the lookout for a warm, cozy place to sleep, a cat can sometimes "go missing" in your own home. It is important to know where its hiding places are and ensure that they are safe. Laundry baskets, linen closets, wardrobes, and drawers are all fair game to cats. Some have a predilection for washing machines and dryers. Keep the door to these appliances closed, and always check for sleeping cats inside before starting them.

MEOW ON COMMAND
Teaching your cat to meow upon hearing its name will make it easier to find it—inside the house or out.

SNUG AND COZY
Cats excel at finding the smallest nooks in which to retire for a little snooze. This kitten has hidden in a school bag.

Sniffing

72 SPRAYING

Like scratching, spraying urine is a way for cats to mark territory. Normally, cats feel secure enough in their home not to display this behavior. However, at times of increased stress—the arrival of a new kitten, for example—a cat (usually male) might spray around the house. Prevent spraying by learning the telltale signs. If your cat still sprays, clean up the affected area with disinfectant to remove the odor.

ABOUT TO SPRAY
Backing up against the chair, this cat is about to spray: its hind legs are on tip toes, and its tail is raised and quivering.

73 IN OR OUT AT NIGHT?

The days of putting the cat out for the night are gone. At nighttime, your cat is more likely to be involved in a fight with another cat or with other predators. In addition, despite there being less traffic at night, it is often faster, representing a serious danger for your cat. For its own safety, keep your cat in after dark. The local wildlife will also benefit from your cat being kept indoors at night.

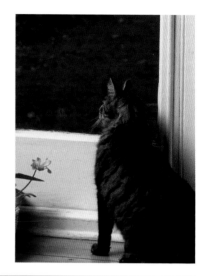

DARKNESS IS NO DETERRENT
With their incredible night vision, cats will still happily venture out after dusk. But many owners prefer to keep their pet in at night.

74 FIRST TIME OUTSIDE

Make sure your cat is confident in the home before letting it out for the first time, and when you do, supervise its first few trips outside. Open the door, step into the yard, and call it gently, maybe waving a feather-stick toy to encourage it to come out. Do not force your cat outside; it will go when it feels ready.

NERVOUS CAT
Cats like being in control of their territory, so being faced with a vast expanse of outdoor space might be daunting at first. They may display fearful behavior, slinking around very close to the ground.

EXPLORING
Cats are natural-born explorers, and the nooks and crannies in your yard will provide them with hours of fun.

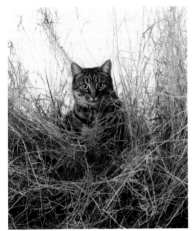

75

THE HUNTING INSTINCT

Cats are fearsome predators, and the hunting instinct is ingrained deep within them. Even domestic cats, which do not have to worry about their next meal, enjoy hunting. For these well-fed cats, hunting is more about the thrill of the chase. This is one theory for why cats play with their prey before killing it.

PATIENT HUNTERS
Hidden in the tall grass, this cat waits patiently for some unsuspecting prey to cross its path.

STALKING
When a cat spots its prey, it approaches slowly, lowering its entire body into a distinctive gait before pouncing.

76

UNWANTED PRESENTS

If your cat is allowed to go out, chances are it will return one day with a little gift for you—a mouse, a bird, or a little frog, often dead, but sometimes alive. As disgusting as this behavior might seem to you, it is important not to reprimand your cat. This gesture is meant out of love, possibly as your cat's humble contribution to the family table. Instead, praise it for its superior hunting skills, then dispose of the prey quickly while your cat is not looking.

PROUD PROVIDER
This cat gives its offering of a dead mouse the way a mother cat presents her kittens with prey. It is a cat's way of showing love and to nurture its human family.

Dead mouse

47

LIVING WITH A CAT

77 READING NEGATIVE BODY LANGUAGE

Flapping tail

Since cats cannot tell us how they feel, it is important to learn to read their body language in order to forge successful relationships. The two most expressive parts of a cat's body are its tail and ears, but its eyes and mouth are also very revealing. While not strictly body language, each of a cat's range of vocal emissions is also key to understanding its state of mind.

Low growl

GROWLING
A feline growl seems to emanate from the pit of the cat's stomach. A growl is a definite warning sign and often a prelude to a fight.

TAIL SWISHING
Do not mistake a cat's swishing tail for friendliness. Unlike dogs, cats wag their tails when they are angry or nervous.

HISSING
A hissing cat, with its ears back and its teeth bared, makes quite a fierce impression. However, a cat hisses when it feels threatened rather than aggressive.

READING POSITIVE BODY LANGUAGE

78

While negative feline body language has been witnessed at some time or other by anybody who shares their life with a cat, much more familiar is a cat's display of positive body language. After all, most family cats are well loved and cared for, face relatively few threats in their daily lives, and are probably relaxed and happy within their home environment. A happy cat can be recognized by a tail held upright, slowly blinking eyes, and ears pointing upward.

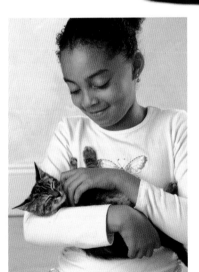

PURRING
Cats purr when they are content and relaxed. However, when they are nervous or distressed, they might also purr as a way to comfort themselves.

KNEADING
Similar to the movements needed to make dough, this padding behavior is based on the action used to encourage a mother's milk and shows your cat feels happy and loved.

NUZZLING
Cats have scent glands in their lips and chin. By rubbing their faces against a littermate or their favorite person, they are effectively claiming it or you as their own.

79

TOYS & PLAY

A vital element of feline development, playtime teaches kittens about social interaction—what is acceptable behavior and what is not, for example—as well as the hunting skills they would need in nature. Playing with your cat strengthens the bond between you. Establish a routine that incorporates 15 or 20 minutes of play time each day. It will keep your cat physically and mentally active—and less likely to develop destructive behavior.

Play glove with hanging toys

Ping-pong ball

CATNIP TOYS

Some cat toys are stuffed with dried catnip, an herb that creates a hormonal reaction in most cats over six months old, giving them a gentle high.

PING PONG

Cats love to chase fast-moving objects, and a lightweight ping-pong ball bouncing around is the perfect toy. Put it away at the end of the playing session to prevent anyone slipping on it.

SWINGING THINGS

A toy hanging on a self-balancing surface will keep your cat thoroughly entertained as it swats at and catches it, re-creating the feeling of chasing live prey.

Cat is focused

Cat bats with its front paws

Tail helps with balance

POUNCING & PLAY FIGHTING
Kittens hone their hunting skills by play fighting with their littermates. They will take turns ambushing each other and engage in seemingly ferocious wrestles.

Surprised by ambushing kitten

Pouncing unexpectedly

Waste paper basket

Feather

Kitten is curious and gentle

HIDE & SEEK
Kittens love playing hide and seek. If possible, provide them with a couple of cardboard boxes from which they can keep an eye on things and ambush at will.

FEATHERS
A feather offers a taste of the excitement of chasing birds. To avoid scratches, use a feather stick, but never leave any cat alone with feathers or with toys that include lengths of string or ribbon.

FELINE FISHING
A dangling toy on a ribbon is a great bait to reel in your cat, which will be unable to resist the quick movement as you flick it above its head. The cat will use all sorts of acrobatic skills to catch its "prey."

51

80 LIVING WITH A TIMID CAT

Some cats enjoy meeting people, while others run and hide when faced with a new person in the house. This could be because they were not socialized properly as kittens. If your cat is timid, give it constant reassurance by speaking to it in a soft and encouraging voice. Do not force it to face whatever is making it nervous.

SAFE CORNER
Position an igloo or a cardboard box with a warm blanket in it in a quiet corner of the house, so your cat can take refuge in it when it feels afraid.

CURIOUS BUT AFRAID
A cat in new surroundings will investigate cautiously at first. Left to sniff around at their own pace, though, most quickly grow in confidence.

81 MOVING

When you move to a new home, even if it is just to the other side of town, keep your cat inside for the first couple of weeks. The homing instinct is strong in cats, and they sometimes try to find their way back to their old territory. Wait until your cat has accepted the new home as its territory before letting it out.

Wicker cat carrier

SAFE TRAVELS
Moving can be chaotic. Keep your cat in its carrier, and do not let it travel in the moving van—take it with you.

82 TRAVELING WITH A CAT

Most cats do not enjoy car trips, not least because for them it means being confined to their carrier. Do not be tempted to allow your cat, no matter how docile, to roam freely in the car. For its own safety and yours, always use its carrier. Line it with a blanket for comfort, and put a few toys in there. If you are embarking on a long journey, stop regularly to allow your cat to take litter breaks and to have some food and water.

1 Put the carrier in an enclosed room with no escape routes. This is because your cat might put up a struggle.

2 When your cat is in, lock the door, making sure not to trap its paws or tail. A favorite towel or blanket will help comfort your cat.

3 Put the carrier on the back seat, ideally with another person holding it steady. If this is not possible, secure it with a seat belt.

83 KENNELS & SITTERS

Make sure your cat is in good hands if you are going away. Neighbors can help, but if you are going away for several days, it might be better to hire a cat sitter or to use a kennel. A cat sitter comes into your home daily to feed and play with the cat and to clean its litter. A kennel is like a hotel for cats, with individual cages offering all the comforts of home. A reputable kennel will expect your cat to be vaccinated before taking it in.

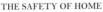

THE SAFETY OF HOME
The advantage of hiring a cat sitter is that your cat is able to remain in its own familiar surroundings.

MULTIPLE-CAT CAGE
Most kennels have cages for single cats, plus a handful of larger ones for two or three cats that are used to living together.

YOUR CAT'S HEALTH

84 SIGNS OF GOOD HEALTH

If you know your cat and its normal behavior well, you will be better able to spot problems early, especially if you also have a regular examination routine. If anything concerns you in terms of the cat's health, call your vet for advice. You may simply be asked to monitor the cat for further developments and to report back. You will probably also be told to take the cat in to see the vet immediately if the condition worsens.

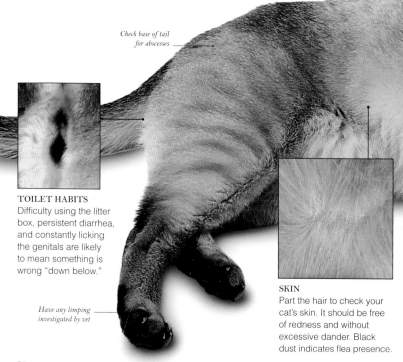

Check base of tail for abscesses

TOILET HABITS
Difficulty using the litter box, persistent diarrhea, and constantly licking the genitals are likely to mean something is wrong "down below."

Have any limping investigated by vet

SKIN
Part the hair to check your cat's skin. It should be free of redness and without excessive dander. Black dust indicates flea presence.

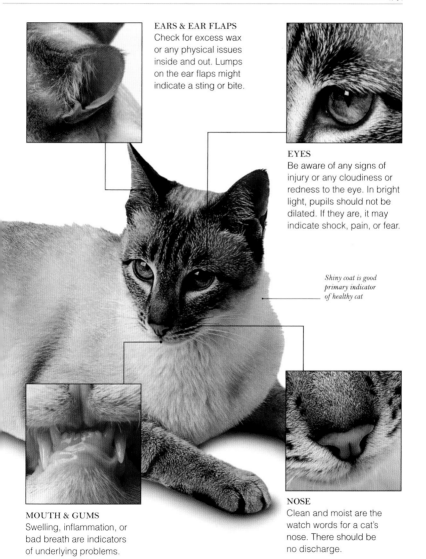

EARS & EAR FLAPS
Check for excess wax or any physical issues inside and out. Lumps on the ear flaps might indicate a sting or bite.

EYES
Be aware of any signs of injury or any cloudiness or redness to the eye. In bright light, pupils should not be dilated. If they are, it may indicate shock, pain, or fear.

Shiny coat is good primary indicator of healthy cat

MOUTH & GUMS
Swelling, inflammation, or bad breath are indicators of underlying problems.

NOSE
Clean and moist are the watch words for a cat's nose. There should be no discharge.

85 CARING FOR AN ELDERLY CAT

A cat that is well looked after can live 15 years or longer. You may need to alter your cat's routine as it enters its twilight years. Its appetite might change, and you may need to feed it more frequently. If this is the case, make its meals smaller. Keep an eye on your cat's toilet habits, as well as on the condition of its coat. Being aware of any changes is the key to catching any age-related problems well in advance.

SLEEPING
Older cats tend to sleep more. They may also be slightly confused upon waking, so try not to disturb them unnecessarily.

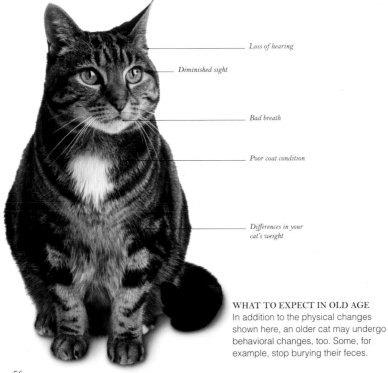

Loss of hearing

Diminished sight

Bad breath

Poor coat condition

Differences in your cat's weight

WHAT TO EXPECT IN OLD AGE
In addition to the physical changes shown here, an older cat may undergo behavioral changes, too. Some, for example, stop burying their feces.

86 CARING FOR A PREGNANT CAT

Although it is advisable to spay your female cat before her first season, there might come a time when you have to deal with a pregnant cat. A feline pregnancy becomes visible at about five weeks, which is roughly halfway through the term. If you are a responsible owner, your cat should already be vaccinated; if she is not, do not vaccinate her during the pregnancy, because this could affect the health of the fetuses. As the pregnancy progresses, your cat will become less active.

CARE CHECKLIST

A pregnant cat will have an increased appetite. Make sure she is well fed, both during and after the pregnancy. Producing milk is hungry business!

Notice where your cat has chosen to nest, and make this area as comfortable as possible. As the pregnancy progresses, she will spend more and more time there, impregnating the bedding with her smell as a beacon for her soon-to-be-born kittens.

Even an inexperienced cat will probably be fine without your help during the delivery. Just sit back and enjoy the show.

Relaxed face

Round belly

KITTENING BOX
You will often find a heavily pregnant cat, also known as a queen, lying down. This is to distribute evenly the weight in her belly.

PROUD MOTHER-TO-BE
This queen proudly displays her pregnant belly. Cats usually give birth to between two and five kittens.

87

CONTROLLING FLEAS, TICKS & WORMS

Treat your cat for fleas regularly, especially during the warm summer months. Since fleas can survive away from the cat, it is also important to treat the home environment. Ticks are blood-sucking parasites that latch onto your cat's skin, especially around the face. Worms are internal parasites that can live in the lungs or the intestines; the best preventive measure is a worming pill every six months.

FLEAS & TICKS

Symptoms: If your cat scratches obsessively, it might have fleas. Part its coat so you can see its skin. Fleas look like tiny brown specks, but the presence of small black droppings is also a sign of an infestation, as is irritated skin. Ticks look and feel like small warts on your cat's skin.

Treatments: Flea treatment is available in the form of several products that are applied to the back of your cat's neck; your home should also be treated. Ticks must be removed manually; it is a tricky task, so ask your vet to explain how.

Flea treatment

EAR MITES

Symptoms: Persistent scratching of and pawing at the ears and vigorous shaking of the head are usually symptoms of an ear mite infestation. Check the inside of your cat's ears for the presence of dark spots and brown waxy discharge. There might also be an unpleasant smell.

Treatments: Flea-treatment products usually eliminate ear mites, too. In the case of severe infestations, your vet might prescribe drops.

Itchy ears

WORMS

Symptoms: There are different symptoms for different types of worm. The lungworm causes breathing problems, such as a persistent cough, while worms that take up residence in your cat's intestines might cause weight loss, diarrhea, and anemia, which reveals itself as pale gums. Worms might also be visible in your cat's stools.

Treatments: Give your cat a worming pill every six months. Some flea-treatment products are also effective in the treatment of worms.

Vet diagnosis

Get the new myVCA app!

- Quickly book appointments
- Get health care and medication reminders
- Easily order your pet's food, treats, medications and more
- Access personalized pet care information

VCA CareClub® Member Exclusives:

- 24/7 live chat with a veterinarian*
- View VCA CareClub member plan details

myVCA

Download It Today!

 AT VCA ANIMAL HOSPITALS, WE CARE

*Live chat is provided exclusively to VCA CareClub members through the myVCA mobile app, available at Apple's App Store and Google Play.

ZOETIS PETCARE
REWARDS

VETHICAL° **Paradyne**°
(selamectin)

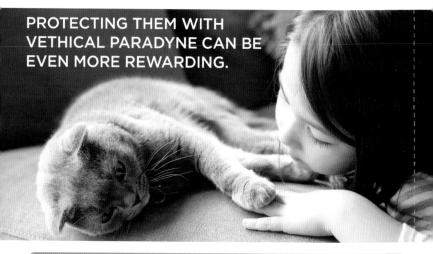

PROTECTING THEM WITH VETHICAL PARADYNE CAN BE EVEN MORE REWARDING.

HOW IT WORKS

 = = $

PURCHASE VETHICAL PARADYNE
Submit a receipt to the Zoetis Petcare Rewards website

POINTS
Earn points for each purchase of Vethical Paradyne

REWARDS
Redeem rewards for a reloadable Visa Prepaid Card to pay for any product or service at your VCA Animal Hospital

To enroll or submit receipts, go to ZoetisPetcareRewards.com

AT VCA ANIMAL HOSPITALS, WE CARE

88 DEALING WITH HAIR BALLS

Cats are fastidiously clean, and daily grooming means that they ingest a surprising amount of their own hair. Most cats will eat a little grass to bring up a hair ball. Specially formulated hair ball-formula cat food is also available. And of course, you can do your bit by brushing your cat regularly.

Self-grooming

ACCUMULATED FUR
Longhaired cats are particularly prone to hair balls, because they inevitably ingest a larger quantity of hair while grooming.

89 NOTICING SIGNS OF DISTRESS

When they are not feeling well, cats have a tendency to hide and isolate themselves rather than seek help or even comfort from their human family. Although in many cases cats are great self-healers, some conditions require veterinary assistance. It is therefore important to recognize the signs that all might not be well.

HIDING AWAY
A normally social cat that suddenly hides and stops interacting with its human family might be unwell.

EATING & DRINKING HABITS
Investigate any changes in your cat's appetite and thirst, since the underlying reasons could be serious, such as diabetes.

UNJUSTIFIED AGGRESSION
If your cat behaves aggressively for seemingly no good reason, it could be because it is in pain. Take it to the vet.

WOUNDS

90

If your cat comes back from its outdoor patrols with an open wound, it might try to behave as if nothing is wrong. This is a natural response in an attempt not to show any weakness. If the wound is on its paw, your cat will likely tuck it in under its body to prevent you from examining it. While minor scratches and abrasions may be treated at home with a cold compress and a bandage, any open wounds should be seen by a vet immediately.

BANDAGING WOUNDS
It is quite difficult to put a bandage on an injured, stressed cat, so you might want to leave this task to the vet.

STINGS

91

Curious explorers, cats sometimes come up against bees and wasps. If your cat has been stung by an insect, the affected area will appear red and swollen. If you see something that resembles a splinter wound, it could be a bee sting. Try to remove it with tweezers. Some cats are allergic to bee stings, and they might develop respiratory difficulties. A visit to the vet is recommended.

A wasp can give a nasty sting

TREATING BITES
Bites usually need just a course of antibiotics to heal. However, sometimes a bite turns into an abscess. This will require lancing.

BITES

92

Even a neutered cat with a diminished territorial drive will have the occasional dispute with a rival. While scratches tend to heal without medical attention, bites can become infected because cats' saliva harbors bacteria that may enter the bloodstream. Venomous spiders or snakes may also be a concern in some parts of the world. If there is a puncture wound on your cat's skin, see your vet immediately.

93

WHEN TO GO TO THE VET

Learning to read the signs of ill health in your cat will prevent unnecessary trips to the vet, which can be stressful for your cat and expensive for you. However, do not hesitate to consult your vet if your cat has a persistent complaint or visible injuries, or if it appears to be in shock or pain.

CHOOSING A VET

The best way to find a vet is by word of mouth. Ask friends and neighbors where they take their pets and whether they are happy with the care they receive there. You can also ask your local shelter where they take their residents for checkups.

At the clinic, ask about their facilities and whether they provide around-the-clock emergency care. Also find out how many vets practice there and whether your cat will see the same one each time.

MEDICAL INSURANCE

Veterinary emergencies are expensive affairs. In addition to the price of treatment, you might have to consider the cost of boarding, since an injured cat may need to be kept overnight for observation.

To help deal with such bills, insure your cat. You may still have to pay your vet up front, but after filing a claim, you should get a large percentage of your money back.

CONFIDENT HANDLING

Vets have a strong, confident way of dealing with animals, and they know how to pacify cats that are in pain or injured.

EMERGENCY CARE

Medical emergencies can happen at any time. Make sure you know the after-hours contact details for your chosen veterinary practice as well as the location, which may be different.

61

94 SYMPTOMS OF ILL HEALTH

Although cats cannot tell us what is wrong with them, their bodies and their behavior speak volumes about their state of health. Anybody who shares their life with a cat will soon get to know what constitutes normal behavior for their feline companion and what is unusual. Keep an eye out for any changes in their appetite, energy levels, and litter-box habits. At least once a week, examine their mouth, ears, and eyes, and check their breath. If anything seems out of the ordinary, consider a trip to the vet.

PALE OR INFLAMED GUMS
The color of your cat's gums is indicative of potential problems. Healthy gums are pale pink.

CHANGE IN EATING HABITS
Monitor your cat's appetite, since any changes could be a sign of ill health. If your cat refuses to eat for more than 24 hours, consult the vet.

STRANGE BEHAVIOR
Cats are creatures of habit. If they suddenly display unusual behavior—howling when they have always been docile, for example—there might be something wrong.

Be aware of difficulty in litter box

LITTER PROBLEMS
Keep on top of any bowel issues and urinary-tract problems by cleaning your cat's litter box regularly. If your cat cries loudly while in its box, it might have a urinary tract infection.

LETHARGY

A lack of interest in everything is a definite cause for concern in cats, especially if it is accompanied by loss of appetite.

LIST OF OTHER SYMPTOMS

See your vet if your cat displays any of the symptoms listed below or, indeed, any signs of ill health.

• **Increased thirst, frequent urination, weight loss, bad breath, and mouth ulcers** are indicators of chronic kidney disease, common in older cats.

• **Vomiting and dehydration** are more in keeping with acute kidney disease, which is more readily seen in younger cats and often caused by an infection.

• **Diarrhea** can be caused by a range of problems, as benign as a food allergy or as serious as feline infectious enteritis.

• **Rapid, labored, or noisy breathing** should be investigated as soon as possible.

• **Limping** can indicate a large range of potential problems, including hard- and soft-tissue injuries, as well as age-related and more serious concerns.

Scratching with hind paw

SCRATCHING

Persistent scratching is probably related to the presence of fleas, ear mites, and other parasites. Check your cat's coat and ears for uninvited guests.

Drooling saliva

Low posture

EXCESSIVE DROOLING

Any unusual drooling is cause for concern. There might be something stuck in your cat's mouth, or it might have ingested a toxic substance. Take it to the vet immediately.

COMMON CAT ILLNESSES

95

Just as in humans, there are myriad ailments, illnesses, and complaints that can affect a cat's various body parts. Some are caught from other cats, while others might be common in certain breeds. The key to the best treatment is to spot issues early. This can best be facilitated through routine handling and checking of your cat, and by knowing what feels and looks normal for it.

Persians (or Longhairs) often have breathing problems

JOINTS

Joint disease can be so mild as to go unnoticed by a pet owner or, at the other extreme, can greatly affect an animal's life. Most cases fall somewhere between the two.

PROBLEM SIGNS

• Limping • Stiffness • Inability to jump • Lack of desire to move • Difficulty climbing stairs • Favoring one leg over another • Displaying signs of discomfort or pain when moving

EYES

Among the most common problems with cats' eyes are conjunctivitis, cataracts, glaucoma, keratitis, and a visible third eyelid. Examine your cat's eyes regularly to ensure all is well.

PROBLEM SIGNS

• Redness • Swelling • Presence of discharge
• Cloudiness • Watering • Opacity of the lens
• Bulging eyes • Tear-stained fur around eyes
• Inflamed cornea • Visible third eyelid

EARS

Infections of the ear can be uncomfortable and should be treated quickly. Ear mites are commonly found and contagious, so treat all your cats at the first sign of infestation.

PROBLEM SIGNS

• Tilted head • Head shaking • Redness/swelling
• Unpleasant odor • Pawing/scratching ear area
• Loss of balance • Sensitive near ears • Discharge
• Dark brown wax • Hearing loss • Bleeding

SKIN & HAIR

A wide range of problems can affect a cat's skin and hair, including bacterial infections, yeast infections, fleas and lice, ringworm, allergic dermatitis, and even alopecia.

PROBLEM SIGNS

• Constant scratching or licking • Hair loss • Blotchy or red skin • Spots around chin • Red ear flap • Lesions • Chewing obsessively at reachable extremities • Black dust in fur • Flaky skin

DIGESTIVE SYSTEM

There are many ailments that can strike at the digestive system. Some of the most common are intestinal obstruction, food poisoning, and anal-sac irritation.

PROBLEM SIGNS

• Diarrhea • Vomiting • Frequent regurgitation • Constipation • Distended belly • Loss of appetite • Obsessive cleaning of anal area • Weight loss • Increased frequency of defecation

RESPIRATORY SYSTEM

Cat flu is a chief cause of sneezing in cats, but see your vet if any discharge is produced. Breathing problems can be caused by physical obstructions or injury, among other things.

PROBLEM SIGNS

• Wheezing • Coughing • Sneezing • Choking • Gagging • Rapid, shallow breathing • Noisy breathing • Difficulty breathing

HEART & BLOOD

From heart disease and blood clots, to thyroid problems and anemia (which may indicate underlying concerns), there is no shortage of issues that can affect a cat's circulatory system. See a vet if you are concerned.

PROBLEM SIGNS

• Lethargy and weakness • Weight loss
• Diminished appetite • Fever • Depression
• Increased heart rate

96 GIVING PILLS & LIQUID MEDICINE

Administering medicine to cats is notoriously difficult because they are usually uncooperative. It is important to get it right the first time because they will become increasingly stressed, which is likely to cause them to lash out with each repeated attempt. If necessary, have somebody help hold your cat still. Mixing crumbled-up pills with the cat's food is a good idea in theory, but cats have a remarkable sense of smell and may detect any anomalies in their bowl.

1 Hold your cat firmly, but not roughly, by the head, without touching its whiskers. Place your index finger and thumb either side of its mouth, and tilt its head back slightly.

2 With the other hand, gently pry your cat's mouth open by pressing on its jaw, and put the pill on the back of your cat's tongue. Close its mouth and massage its throat.

LIQUID MEDICINE
If your vet prescribes liquid medicine, administer it with a syringe. Hold the cat's head still with one hand but do not tilt it back, then slowly squirt the liquid into the side of its mouth.

97 GIVING EYE DROPS

Your cat's eyes should be clear of any discharge before you apply eye drops, so clean the area around them with a ball of moistened cotton. Squeeze the eye drops into the eye, then close the eyelid for a few seconds, to allow the drops to spread evenly on the cornea. Apply eye drops or eye ointment to your cat's eyes only if you have been instructed to do so by your vet.

HOLD STILL
Hold your cat's head still in the same way that you would when administering a pill (see Tip 96). Your cat might struggle—be sure not to scratch its eye with the nozzle.

98 GIVING EAR DROPS

If your cat is suffering from an ear mite infection, a course of ear drops will be prescribed. Before starting, wipe away any visible dirt from the affected area with a piece of moistened cotton. Gently hold your cat's head (see Tip 96), tilting it so that the ear to be treated is pointing upward slightly. Apply the drops, then massage them gently into the ear.

CAREFUL ADMINISTRATION
As always with cats, it is important to be firm but gentle. Do not insert the dropper into the ears, which are extremely delicate.

99 CARING FOR A SICK CAT

If your cat is sick or recovering from an injury, it will need a little extra care. Help your cat regain its strength by making a sick bed for it. A cardboard box lined with soft blankets should do the trick. Position it in a quiet corner, away from drafts and foot traffic.

Lukewarm hot-water bottle

Elizabethan collar

EXTRA COZY
Make your cat's bed more appealing than ever by putting a hot-water bottle full of lukewarm water under a towel or blanket.

SCRATCH PREVENTION
If your cat has received an injury and has been given stitches, an Elizabethan collar will prevent it from bothering them.

100 FEEDING A SICK CAT

A sick cat might have to be on a special diet, which it will probably find unappetizing, or it might reject its food altogether. There are a few tricks to get your cat to eat—from serving its favorite food, to spoon-feeding nourishing liquid food.

FOOD FOR SICK CATS
A sick or recovering cat needs to be kept well nourished. Try feeding it smaller meals than usual. If your cat enjoys fresh food, such as fish or chicken, prepare some. Serve the food warm because this will activate the smell, making it more pungent and appetizing. If all else fails, you might have to syringe-feed your cat some liquefied high-protein food.

SPOON-FEEDING YOUR CAT
Hold your cat's head in the way shown in Tip 96. Spoon-feed it some unsalted chicken stock or liquefied convalescent cat food.

101

HUMAN HEALTH ISSUES

The most common cat-related human health issue is an allergy. A cat allergy manifests itself with red, itchy eyes, sneezing, and a tickly throat. Some people also develop skin rashes, especially if they get scratched. It is, however, possible to build up a resistance to a cat allergy, and there are also hypoallergenic cat breeds. Other, more serious conditions include rabies and toxoplasmosis.

Beware of cat bites

RABIES
Rabies is carried in some animals' saliva. In countries where rabies is present, even the most innocuous cat bite should be taken seriously.

ALLERGIES
People who are allergic to cats display a range of symptoms that usually affect the respiratory system.

Wash your hands thoroughly

Use rubber gloves

TOXOPLASMOSIS
Cat droppings may contain a parasite that causes a range of diseases, including skin infections and toxoplasmosis. The latter is a greater risk for pregnant women. Wear rubber gloves when cleaning your cat's litter and wash your hands thoroughly afterward.

69

INDEX

A

abdomen, health checks
  22–3
abscesses 60
Abyssinian 12
adult cats 9, 10
  health checks 23
  settling in 25
aggression 44, 59
ailments 60
allergies 13, 69

B

baskets 18, 68
bathing cats 40
bedding 18, 68
begging 44
birth 57
bites 60
blood diseases 65
body language 28, 48–9
body shapes 13
boredom 10, 44
bowls 18, 32, 33
breathing problems 63, 65
breeders 14, 26
breeds 12
British Shorthair 12
brushes 20, 35, 36
buying cats 14

C

call signs 26
cancer 38
car travel 53
carriers 20, 53
cat flaps 19, 41
cat flu 65
cat sitters 53
catnip 50
children 24, 29

choosing a cat 8–11
claws
  clipping 20, 39
  declawing 39
  scratching 42
  scratching posts 21, 42
coat 13
  grooming 35–6
  health checks 22–3
  problems 65
combs 35, 36
Cornish Rex 12, 13
crossbreeds 9

D

declawing 39
Devon Rex 12, 13
diarrhea 54, 58, 63
digestive problems 65
dogs 29
drooling 63
dry food 30, 32

E

ears
  cleaning 38
  ear drops 67
  health checks 22–3, 55
  mites 38, 58, 63
  problems 64
elderly cats 56
Elizabethan collars 68
equipment 18–21
eyes
  cleaning 37
  eye drops 67
  health checks 22–3, 55
  problems 64
  shapes 13
  third eyelid 37

F

face
  nuzzling 49
  shapes 13
feeding bowls 18, 32, 33
female cats 10
  spaying 10, 27
feral cats 15
fights 46, 51, 60
fleas 54, 58, 63
food 30–3
  begging 44
  equipment 18
  fussy eaters 33
  milk 31
  overfeeding 33
  pregnant cats 57
  routines 32
  sick cats 68
  treats 31, 43
  wet and dry food 30
foreign bodies 37, 38
fur see coat
fussy eaters 33

G

gardens 17
grass, eating 34
grooming
  bathing 40
  equipment 20
  longhaired cats 35
  shorthaired cats 36
growling 48
gums, health 22–3, 62

H

hair balls 34, 35, 59
hairless cats 13
handling cats 28, 29
health care 58–69

health checks 22–3, 54–5
heart problems 65
Himalayan 37
hissing 48
home
  cat-proofing 16
  moving 52
hunting 47, 51

I J
illness 27, 59, 62–9
indoor cats 11, 12
insect stings 60
insurance, health 61
joint disease 64

K
kennels 53
kidney disease 63
kittens 9
  birth 57
  health checks 22
  litter training 41
  milk 31
  play 12, 50–1
  settling in 24
  vaccinations 27
kneading 49

L
legal responsibilities 11
legs, health checks 22–3
lethargy 63
limping 63
litter boxes 19, 54, 62
litter training 41
Longhair *see* Persian
longhaired cats 13
  hair balls 34, 35, 59
  grooming 35

M
Maine Coon 9
male cats 10
  neutering 9, 10, 12, 27, 43
meat 32
medical problems 58–69
medicines 66–7

meowing 45
microchips 15, 27
milk 31
missing cats 45
mites 38, 58, 63
mouth, health checks 22–3, 55, 62
moving home 52

N
names 26
negative body language 48
neutering 9, 10, 12, 27, 43
nighttime 46
no-go areas 42
nose, health checks 22–3, 55
nuzzling 49

O
obesity 33
outdoor cats 11
overfeeding 33

P
pain 59
parasites 38, 58, 63
paws
  health checks 22–3
  kneading 49
  scent glands 42
  see also claws
Persian 12, 37, 64
picking up a cat 28
pills 66
plants, poisonous 16, 17, 34
play 12, 21, 50–1
poisons 16, 17
positive body language 49
pregnancy 57, 69
prey, hunting 47
purebred cats 9, 14
purring 49

R
rabies 69
Ragdoll 12
rescue shelters 14, 25, 26
respiratory problems 63, 65
rewards 26, 43

S
safety 16, 46
scent glands 42, 49
scratching 42, 63
scratching posts 21, 42
Selkirk Rex 13
shorthaired cats 13, 36
Siamese 12
Siberian Forest 14
sick cats 68
skin
  health checks 54
  problems 65
sleep 18, 42, 56
socialization 8, 29, 52
spaying 10, 27
Sphynx 13
spoon-feeding 68
spraying 45
stings 60
stray cats 15, 43
stroking 36
syringes 66

T
tails, body language 48, 49
tear ducts 37
teeth, brushing 20, 40
ticks 58
timid cats 52
toothbrushes 40
toothpaste 40
toxoplasmosis 69
toys 21, 50–1
training cats 26
travel 20, 53
treats 31, 43

U V W Y
urinary tract infections 62
urine, spraying 45
vacations 53
vaccinations 27, 57
vets 61
water, drinking 31
wet food 30
worms 58
wounds 60, 68
yards 17, 46

ACKNOWLEDGMENTS

Sands Publishing Solutions would like to thank
Kim Bryan for her efficient consultancy work during the project,
as well as for her assistance in fine-tuning the contents at the outset;
Natalie Godwin for design assistance; and the ever-brilliant Hilary Bird
for making such swift work of the index.

Dorling Kindersley would like to thank the following photographers:
Paul Bricknell, Jane Burton, Steve Gorton, Anna Hall, Mark Henrie,
Dave King, Alison Logan, Steve Lyne, Tracy Morgan, Gary Ombler,
Tim Ridley, Paul Self, and Tracy Morgan Animal Photography.

Picture credits
11 cr: Sylvia Tombesi-Walton
15 r: Cheuk-king Lo. Pearson Education Asia Ltd.
24 bl: kitten courtesy of The Mayhew Animal Home and Humane Education Centre
42 br: Sylvia Tombesi-Walton
49 bl: kitten courtesy of Betty

All other images © Dorling Kindersley.
For further information, see www.dkimages.com

Paradyne® (selamectin)
Topical Parasiticide For Dogs and Cats

CAUTION:
US Federal law restricts this drug to use by or on the order of a licensed veterinarian.

DESCRIPTION:
Paradyne (selamectin) Topical Parasiticide is available as a colorless to yellow, ready to use solution in single dose tubes for topical (dermal) treatment of dogs six weeks of age and older and cats eight weeks of age and older. The content of each tube is formulated to provide a minimum of 2.7 mg/lb (6 mg/kg) of body weight of selamectin. The chemical composition of selamectin is (5Z,25S)-25-cyclohexyl-4'-O-de(2,6-dideoxy-3-O-methyl-α-L-$arabino$-hexopyranosyl)-5-demethoxy-25-de (1-methylpropyl)-22,23-dihydro-5-hydroxyiminoavermectin A_{1a}.

INDICATIONS:
Paradyne is recommended for use in dogs six weeks of age or older and cats eight weeks of age and older for the following parasites and indications:

Dogs:
Paradyne kills adult fleas and prevents flea eggs from hatching for one month and is indicated for the prevention and control of flea infestations *(Ctenocephalides felis)*, prevention of heartworm disease caused by *Dirofilaria immitis*, and the treatment and control of ear mite *(Otodectes cynotis)* infestations. Paradyne also is indicated for the treatment and control of sarcoptic mange *(Sarcoptes scabiei)* and for the control of tick infestations due to *Dermacentor variabilis*.

Cats:
Paradyne kills adult fleas and prevents flea eggs from hatching for one month and is indicated for the prevention and control of flea infestations *(Ctenocephalides felis)*, prevention of heartworm disease caused by *Dirofilaria immitis*, and the treatment and control of ear mite *(Otodectes cynotis)* infestations. Paradyne is also indicated for the treatment and control of roundworm *(Toxocara cati)* and intestinal hookworm *(Ancylostoma tubaeforme)* infections in cats.

WARNINGS:
Not for human use. Keep out of the reach of children.

In humans, Paradyne may be irritating to skin and eyes. Reactions such as hives, itching and skin redness have been reported in humans in rare instances. Individuals with known hypersensitivity to Paradyne should use the product with caution or consult a health care professional. Paradyne contains isopropyl alcohol and the preservative butylated hydroxytoluene (BHT). Wash hands after use and wash off any product in contact with the skin immediately with soap and water. If contact with eyes occurs, then flush eyes copiously with water. In case of ingestion by a human, contact a physician immediately. The material safety data sheet (MSDS) provides more detailed occupational safety information. For a copy of the MSDS or to report adverse reactions attributable to exposure to this product, call 1-800-916-8305.

Flammable - Keep away from heat, sparks, open flames or other sources of ignition.

Do not use in sick, debilitated or underweight animals (see SAFETY).

PRECAUTIONS:
Prior to administration of Paradyne, dogs should be tested for existing heartworm infections. At the discretion of the veterinarian, infected dogs should be treated to remove adult heartworms. Paradyne is not effective against adult *D. immitis* and, while the number of circulating microfilariae may decrease following treatment, Paradyne is not effective for microfilariae clearance.

Hypersensitivity reactions have not been observed in dogs with patent heartworm infections administered three times the recommended dose of Paradyne. Higher doses were not tested.

ADVERSE REACTIONS:
Pre-approval clinical trials:
Following treatment with Paradyne, transient localized alopecia with or without inflammation at or near the site of application was observed in approximately 1% of 691 treated cats. Other signs observed rarely ($\leq$0.5% of 1743 treated cats and dogs) included vomiting, loose stool or diarrhea with or without blood, anorexia, lethargy, salivation, tachypnea, and muscle tremors.

Post-approval experience:
In addition to the aforementioned clinical signs that were reported in pre-approval clinical trials, there have been reports of pruritus, urticaria, erythema, ataxia, fever, and rare reports of death. There have also been rare reports of seizures in dogs (see **WARNINGS**).

DOSAGE:

The recommended minimum dose is 2.7 mg selamectin per pound (6 mg/kg) of body weight.

Administer the entire contents of a single dose tube (or two tubes used in combination for dogs weighing over 130 pounds) of Paradyne topically in accordance with the following tables. (See **ADMINISTRATION** for the recommended treatment intervals.)

Cats (lb)	Package color	mg per tube	Potency (mg/mL)	Administered volume (mL)
5.1–15	Teal	45 mg	60	0.75
15.1–22	Taupe	60 mg	60	1.0

For cats over 22 lbs use the appropriate combination of tubes.

Dogs (lb)	Package color	mg per tube	Potency (mg/mL)	Administered volume (mL)
5.1–10	Blue	30 mg	120	0.25
10.1–20	Green	60 mg	120	0.5
20.1–40	Gold	120 mg	120	1.0
40.1–85	Red	240 mg	120	2.0
85.1–130	Purple	360 mg	120	3.0

For dogs over 130 lbs use the appropriate combination of tubes.
Recommended for use in dogs 6 weeks of age and older and in cats 8 weeks of age and older.

ADMINISTRATION:

A veterinarian or veterinary technician should demonstrate or instruct the pet owner regarding the appropriate technique for applying Paradyne topically to dogs and cats prior to first use.

Firmly press the cap down to puncture the seal on the Paradyne tube; a clicking sound will confirm that the cap has successfully punctured the seal. Remove the cap and check to ensure that the tip of the tube is open. To administer the product, part the hair on the back of the animal at the base of the neck in front of the shoulder blades until the skin is visible. Place the tip of the tube on the skin and squeeze the tube 3 or 4 times to empty its entire contents directly onto the skin in one spot. Keeping the tube squeezed, drag it away from the liquid and lift to remove. Check the tube to ensure that it is empty. Do not massage the product into the skin. Due to alcohol content, do not apply to broken skin. Avoid contact between the product and fingers. Do not apply when the haircoat is wet. Bathing or shampooing the animal 2 or more hours after treatment will not reduce the effectiveness of Paradyne. Stiff hair, clumping of hair, hair discoloration, or a slight powdery residue may be observed at the treatment site in some animals. These effects are temporary and do not affect the safety or effectiveness of the product. Discard empty tubes in your ordinary household refuse.

Flea Control in Dogs and Cats

For the prevention and control of flea infestations, Paradyne should be administered at monthly intervals throughout the flea season, starting one month before fleas become active. In controlled laboratory studies >98% of fleas were killed within 36 hours. Results of clinical field studies using Paradyne monthly demonstrated >90% control of flea infestations within 30 days of the first dose. Dogs and cats treated with Paradyne, including those with pre-existing flea allergy dermatitis, showed improvement in clinical signs associated with fleas as a direct result of eliminating the fleas from the animals and their environment.

If the dog or cat is already infested with fleas when the first dose of Paradyne is administered, adult fleas on the animal are killed and no viable fleas hatch from eggs after the first administration. However, an environmental infestation of fleas may persist for a short time after beginning treatment with Paradyne because of the emergence of adult fleas from pupae.

Heartworm Prevention in Dogs and Cats

For the prevention of heartworm disease, Paradyne must be administered on a monthly basis. Paradyne may be administered year-round or at least within one month after the animal's first exposure to mosquitoes and monthly thereafter until the end of the mosquito season. The final dose must be given within one month after the last exposure to mosquitoes. If a dose is missed and a monthly interval between dosing is exceeded then immediate administration of Paradyne and resumption of monthly dosing will minimize the opportunity for the development of adult heartworms. When replacing another heartworm preventive product in a heartworm disease prevention program, the first dose of Paradyne must be given within a month of the last dose of the former medication.

Selamectin, the active ingredient in Paradyne, is a macrocyclic lactone compound. These compounds effectively prevent the development of adult heartworms when administered to dogs and cats within one month of exposure to infective (L_3) *Dirofilaria immitis* larvae. Efficacy of macrocyclic lactones decreases below 100% in dogs, however, if first administered >2 months after exposure to infective larvae. Thus, in heartworm endemic regions, delaying initiation of heartworm prevention using Paradyne beyond 2 months of first exposure to infective larvae (e.g., starting puppies and kittens at >8 weeks of age), or gaps of >2 months in the administration of Paradyne during periods of heartworm transmission, increases the risk of the animal acquiring heartworms. Animals with unknown heartworm history that test negative for heartworms prior to the initiation of Paradyne may be harboring pre-patent infections at the time Paradyne was started. Testing such animals 3–4 months after initiation of Paradyne would be necessary to confirm their negative heartworm status.

At the discretion of the veterinarian, cats ≥6 months of age may be tested to determine the presence of existing heartworm infections before beginning treatment with Paradyne. Cats already infected with adult heartworms can be given Paradyne monthly to prevent further infections.

Ear Mite Treatment in Dogs and Cats

For the treatment of ear mite *(O. cynotis)* infestations in dogs and cats, Paradyne should be administered once as a single topical dose. A second monthly dose may be required in some dogs. Monthly use of Paradyne will control any subsequent ear mite infestations. In the clinical field trials ears were not cleaned, and many animals still had debris in their ears after the second dose. Cleansing of the infested ears is recommended to remove the debris.

Sarcoptic Mange Treatment in Dogs

For the treatment of sarcoptic mange *(S. scabiei)* in dogs, Paradyne should be administered once as a single topical dose. A second monthly dose may be required in some dogs. Monthly use of Paradyne will control any subsequent sarcoptic mange mite infestations. Because of the difficulty in finding sarcoptic mange mites on skin scrapings, effectiveness assessments also were based on resolution of clinical signs. Resolution of the pruritus associated with the mite infestations was observed in approximately 50% of the dogs 30 days after the first treatment and in approximately 90% of the dogs 30 days after the second monthly treatment.

Tick Control in Dogs

For the control of tick *(Dermacentor variabilis)* infestations in dogs, Paradyne should be administered on a monthly basis. In heavy tick infestations, complete efficacy may not be achieved after the first dose. In these cases, one additional dose may be administered two weeks after the previous dose, with monthly dosing continued thereafter.

Nematode Treatment in Cats

For the treatment and control of intestinal hookworm *(A. tubaeforme)* and roundworm *(T. cati)* infections, Paradyne should be applied once as a single topical dose.

SAFETY:
Paradyne has been tested safe in over 100 different pure and mixed breeds of healthy dogs and over 15 different pure and mixed breeds of healthy cats, including pregnant and lactating females, breeding males and females, puppies six weeks of age and older, kittens eight weeks of age and older, and avermectin-sensitive collies. A kitten, estimated to be 5–6 weeks old (0.3 kg), died 8 $\frac{1}{2}$ hours after receiving a single treatment of Paradyne at the recommended dosage. The kitten displayed clinical signs which included muscle spasms, salivation and neurological signs. The kitten was a stray with an unknown history and was malnourished and underweight (see **WARNINGS**).

DOGS: In safety studies, Paradyne was administered at 1, 3, 5, and 10 times the recommended dose to six-week-old puppies, and no adverse reactions were observed. The safety of Paradyne administered orally also was tested in case of accidental oral ingestion. Oral administration of Paradyne at the recommended topical dose in 5- to 8-month-old beagles did not cause any adverse reactions. In a pre-clinical study selamectin was dosed orally to ivermectin-sensitive collies. Oral administration of 2.5, 10, and 15 mg/kg in this dose escalating study did not cause any adverse reactions; however, eight hours after receiving 5 mg/kg orally, one avermectin-sensitive collie became ataxic for several hours, but did not show any other adverse reactions after receiving subsequent doses of 10 and 15 mg/kg orally. In a topical safety study conducted with avermectin-sensitive collies at 1, 3 and 5 times the recommended dose of Paradyne, salivation was observed in all treatment groups, including the vehicle control. Paradyne also was administered at 3 times the recommended dose to heartworm infected dogs, and no adverse effects were observed.

CATS: In safety studies, Paradyne was applied at 1, 3, 5, and 10 times the recommended dose to six-week-old kittens. No adverse reactions were observed. The safety of Paradyne administered orally also was tested in case of accidental oral ingestion. Oral administration of the recommended topical dose of Paradyne to cats caused salivation and intermittent vomiting. Paradyne also was applied at 4 times the recommended dose to patent heartworm infected cats, and no adverse reactions were observed.

In well-controlled clinical studies, Paradyne was used safely in animals receiving other frequently used veterinary products such as vaccines, anthelmintics, antiparasitics, antibiotics, steroids, collars, shampoos and dips.

STORAGE CONDITIONS: Store below 30°C (86°F).

HOW SUPPLIED: Available in seven separate dose strengths for dogs and cats of different weights (see **DOSAGE**). Paradyne for cats and dogs is available in cartons containing 6 single dose tubes.

Paradyne®
(selamectin)

Distributed by:
Vicar Operating, Inc.
12401 West Olympic Blvd.
Los Angeles, CA 90064

Manufactured by:
Zoetis Inc.
Kalamazoo, MI 49007

www.vethical.com

October 2014